Fables Foibles & Other 'Merican Sins

Amoja Sumler

AQUARIUS PRESS
Detroit, Michigan

Copyright © 2020 by Amoja Sumler

All rights reserved. No part of this publication may be reproduced, distributed, or transmitted in any form or by any means, including photocopying, recording, or other electronic or mechanical methods, without the prior written permission of the publisher, except in the case of brief quotations embodied in critical reviews and certain other noncommercial uses permitted by copyright law.

Editor: Randall Horton

ISBN 978-1-7348273-9-2

Aquarius Press LLC
PO Box 23096
Detroit, MI 48223

Willow Books Imprint, www.WillowLit.net

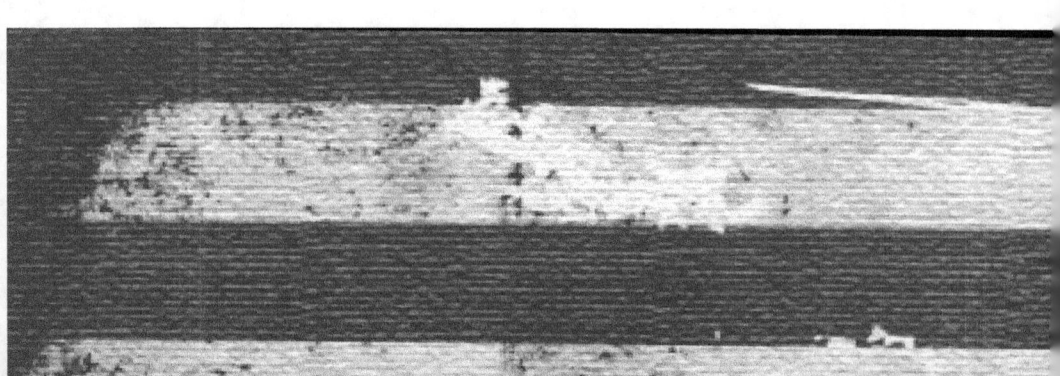

"There is no justice in America,

    but

        it's

           the

              fight

for justice that sustains you."

Baba Amiri Baraka

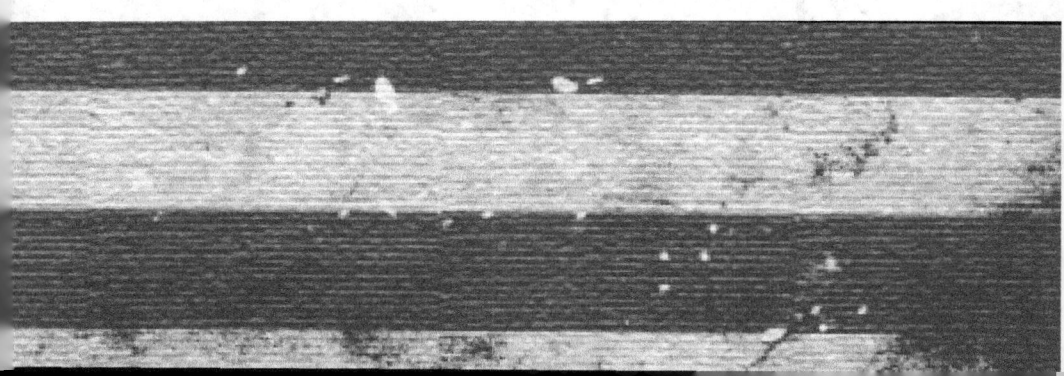

To all the wild hood youngins
        the world over.
                May your neck
                          ever avoid

    their noose.

You are the word made flesh.

fables

johnson puller	15
guernica still	16
prayer to pele	17
money	18
the road to damascus	19
shades of a dutchman	21
lycanthrope	23
icarus asserts	24
abaddon	25
blue stars	27
tecumseh's invocation	28
ozy	30
arse: poetica	31

foibles

another round	37
conductor	38
chrysalis	39
circus carnie	40
the boy (after marie)	42
big timers, ar	43
robbed twice	45
still	47
dissolved girl	48
dew of heaven	49
playlist she will never hear	50
legends and longing	52
as if (a fuckboi rebuke)	53
what i wanted…	54
the offering	55

other 'merican sins

adjudication chamber	59
carolina blood magic	60
language lessons	62
peace be? (for nikki)	64
the key to hitting (after k.r.i.t.)	67
amber's song (with young m.a.)	69
brown's legacy	70
boudin in goshen	72
expiration date	74
who gets words	75
robert johnson's admonition to scratch legba (at the crossroads)	77
colophon	80
artist bio	82

Introduction

In every age a voice calls out. This one is a war horn wailing, a wind whipping up a howl and fanning the flames, invoking an incendiary ancestor, stretching two whole generations back for Amiri Baraka's breath and finding it hot and stank from so much truth telling. *Fables, Foibles, & Other 'Merican Sins* will come for you, still warm from being steeped in Black liberation vapors. With poems like "shades of a dutchman" evoking the same subway car setting as LeRoi Jones' controversial play *Dutchman*, solicitation becomes chastisement and his neo-Clay earns the rebuke "Wassa matter? / You don't like White girls?" He is "immune to the rail buzz" and to the woman, however.

Call them freedom fighters slinging molotovs, or fiery-tongued revolutionaries lit well and flickering, or call them poems. Like a California lightning strike or grown-ass man flint "so fierce and fire full" they start blazes with familiar colloquial licks like

> "Hey lil mama! Wut dat
> mouf do?" A new kind
> of energy, propelling thick
> thighs that love
> each other enough to touch.

They interrupt the dark opening section with the subtlety of a Roman candle. Every institution has fingers pointing at flames threatening to burn it down, and the prurient and patriarchal will be the first to go.

In the second section we are reminded that every poet has loved and lost. This collection holds those "foibles" in its tender middle, in its heart place beneath musical refrains like "Girl I want you but I don't need you," tucked in poems like "still" that reek from the lies unrequited love makes one tell, to "playlist she will never hear" blindly insisting that "this ain't about her./ I want not to miss her, I do;/ I want not to tell her. I do not."

Even as this collection treads into a variety of intimacies and matters of the heart, this is not a book of love poems. These are millennial torches. You will want to fan these pages and watch them burn, even before America catches fire in the final section, finally being judged for "sins" all too familiar to southern Black male backs and necks and hearts.

The poems "adjudication chamber" and "language lessons" anchor the collection, allowing Sumler to scorch the classic Dylan Thomas poem and reconstruct it to create what could be the new national anthem for the moment in which we find ourselves. The chilling refrain that steadies the poem down to its final lines, "Do not go passive when you hear the guns./ Rage, rage against the killing of our sons." still speaks, like Thomas' to those facing death, but goes further to excoriate the in-justice system with lines like, "Though juried men fail us one by one," "good people listen in: verdict stuns," and "left street dead in court's adjourn." With direct and subtle references that call up deaths reaching back to Trayvon Martin, who "stood his ground (lesson learned)" and Eric Garner, "We're barely able to breathe—concerns" the poem rises to uphold the condemnation of America and honors the urgency echoed in Baraka's call that "We have the responsibility to carry the fire, be it in our stomachs or on the end of torches." Sumler offers us both in this timely and necessary collection.

—Frank X Walker

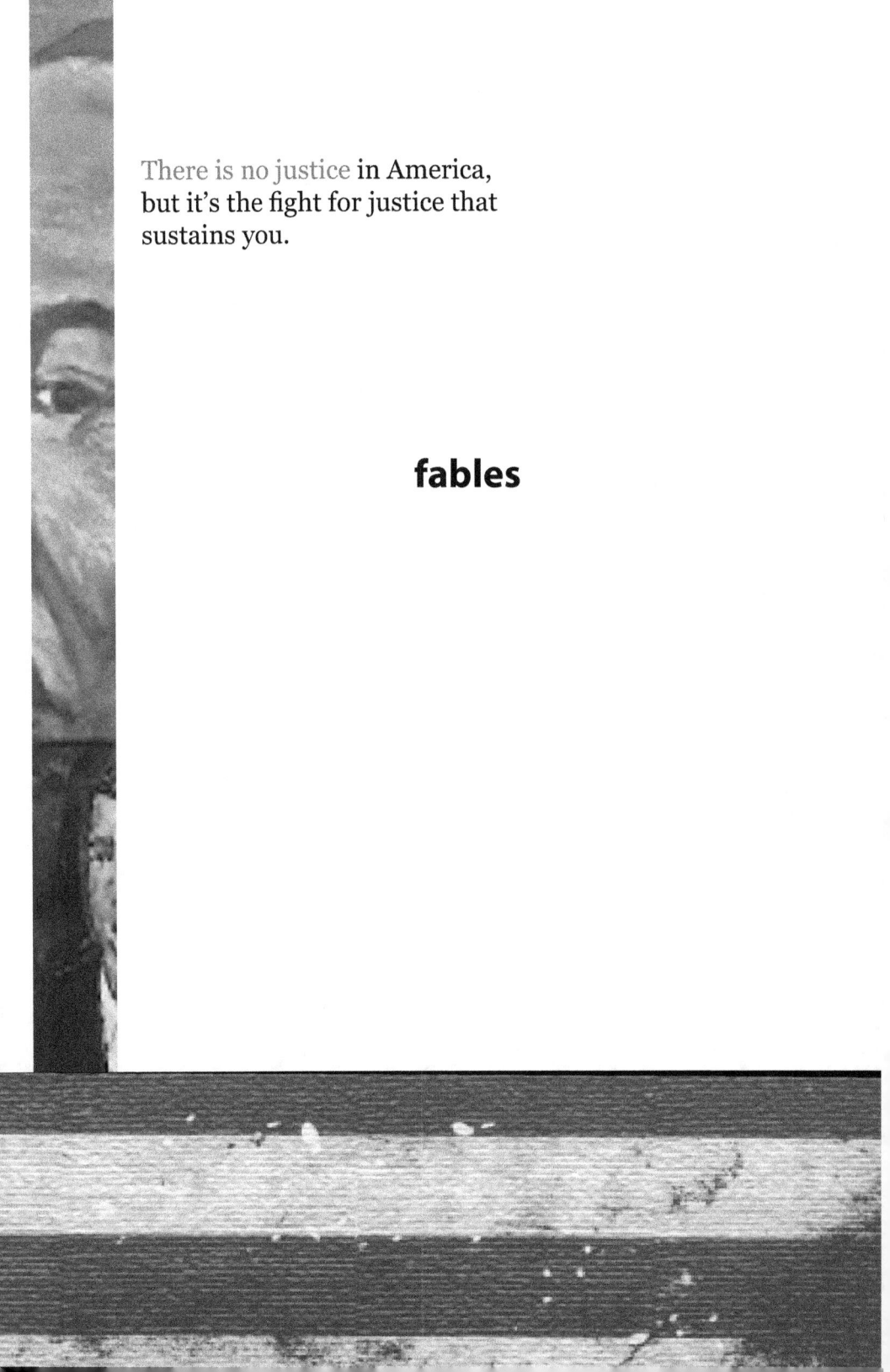

There is no justice in America, but it's the fight for justice that sustains you.

fables

johnson puller

What new
can a poor
Black boi
say about
Papa Scratch Legba?

    Trickster? Changling?
    Johnson puller?
    Crooked lawyer
    from cross
    the road?

Young, old
as time.
Got them
deals. You
trying to
get on?

    Holla
    at a Nicca
    Sign right.
    Here.

guernica still

82 years have died and we're still
lost in this labyrinth of fauna,
Faust, and horses falling
from the sky.
The bombs have left
the plains of Spain and stay
mainly over Baghdad.

        Look. How you Sisyphus?

82 years have died and we're still –
swinging like fascist flags
flying like good and proud boys.
Even now printing presses might
have need for favors and foibles plucked
from Foucault's imagination.
We are the failing of even
your most afeared phobias.

Look. How you symbol us still.

        82 years have died, since they flat

earthed your canvas. Even now
the oil's a surrealist – soiling
U.S. (Black & White)
into a rubix'ed brown spill.

82 years since your
wrist broke from the weight
of prophecy and the Pan(demonium).
of the inks you curdled into a cubing.

prayer to pele

As the helicopter holds me
I offer this prayer (a soft exhale of awe).

Dear awakened broken mountain
matron release your angry earthcore.
Spitting mother devoid of cool
rebuker of couth is it time:
beget a renaming?
In the name of Haulili
I beseech your gush.
Allow me the admiration
of your advance – shrivel
the green unprepared for you.
River your lava through shale teeth.

When the wrath of your work
has frozen a blaze of glossy
obsidian and jagged scoria, I shall gather
your jewels, a blessed fruit of soot
and soil a reminder of your majesty.
Empty your crater
until the oceans boil:
beat and retreating. Ku and Kane
witness my words, Kuahana
run before us dear fetcher of souls.

money

Wall Street magicians summon
      pluck from thin air, like air; hoard
like heaven; keep tucked
away like big dick; in case
      of emergency   raise rates.
P r i c e   j u s t   w e n t   up –
poor Jorge, poor Jimma, broke Betty, all
dance like minstrels for dolla dolla, shake
junk for trickle down, break ground and pull
coal from earthbelly like plasma from vein,
profane bodies and fight like cocks
in an octagon. Cogs barter, beg, and
borrow from bankers busy   b e g i n n i n g
a n e w r o u n d   of   a b r a c a d a b r a.

road to damascus

"Sin sneaks up on you!"

See him? Hands elevated,
like them colored boys
in the presence of authority.
Bible in one hand, rolled Raleigh Durham
in the other, possessed of the Spirit;
ministry spewing like cigarette smoke
from stained lips spitting that gospel.
Sucking that tar in.

His eyes blazing
like the cherry's sizzle,
like his pressed suit,
like hate (his-sing) out each pause:
a new minty fire for his belly.

"Sin hides where you fear to look!"

A bellow to the coals,
an eye open, stoked
for the blush of the burning –
a soul on fire.

The words of Jesus
a too cool candy –
a lure for chir'ren
spit jagged
silky deadly web.
Sure as his daddy
(who Arts in heaven)
aiming to bring
down a buck.

Sure as Hell.
Sure as deft fingers'
flicking the butt away.

His mouth full of
'A man shall not lie with',
Deuteronomy
full of country ham and condemnation;
full of lust for a lucky strike.
Full of shit.

The bulging urge, tucked and folded
away. Sure as an-out-
of-water, sun stroked Paul
himself in a suddenly Jesus
filled desert near Damascus
Arkansas.

shades of a dutchman

Jane sits aloof
antsy from the track's
rattle. A boy sits nearby
immune to the rail buzz
of the sub car.

Sub: a lessor something

Jane sees kinky hair
unlocks legs: imagines
Mandingo.

Jane smirks at
thought of thottery.

Jane sees a shade shaped like a boy –
but smoke don't show them scars.

Jane summons "Hey! Sir? Boy! You?"

Smoke doesn't show
bit lip
– Bloody
Tongue the beautiful.
Jane projects limber dick, swinging

hard as a daddy's disapproval.

Jane envisions a violence
brought her knife and assumptive
pussy ready for either? Both. Yes!

What they say 'bout them smoke boys?

The boy sits cross
legged; inserts ear buds,
practices a calm Jane
bends to piss upon
pulling at his buds

"Hey! Whatcha playing?
Wassa matter? You don't
like White girls?"

lycanthrope

"Hey lil mama! Wut dat
mouf do?" A new kind
of energy, propelling thick
thighs that love
each other enough to touch.

A summer sun races
her to setting round
the way. She's dressed
for it, equal parts bounce
and swish. Hot enough
to get sweated by all the hood
Nicca's hoping for a dip
in her pool.

Pretty
new to this earth,
but hip to the shiz –
I ain't studying them fools.
casting a bare
glance back at Leroy
who has transformed
from homie to howl.

icarus asserts

'No one expecting plummet
takes to the skies.'

My arms waxed
      burned map
           to that fist
                still bleeding
My heart worn
    speed bag
        handled deftly
            risky racer
        slow dodger
    premonition ignorer

My face
skull place
      a broken fountain of salt
            Ex receptacle
                of kisses.
      Scorn bringer

My body popped
    balloon
        air swallower
            crater maker
      bitter bandicoot
    (crash)
        Snort seeker
Her love Summer
    ender jagged
        membrane melter
            feather stealer
      golden orbed
           Death bringer
Gravity has the final say.

abbadon

She calls and I transform,
a new kind of parlor trick
old as every story ever pulped.

A toy in her closet.
Favored, she says.

I am a box of opposites.
So fierce and fire full –
sharp edges:
a breakable thing.

I fear a forgetting.

Her words
billow a stiff chilly wind,
bellow into my Blackness –
below all of the places
I ever hoped to hide.

Her sight leaves me shaken
a site witnessed bare as the cupboards
of my childhood.

This poor kid never
forgot how to hunger.

My defense's whisper
her "Abaddon"
the demon angel of my undoing.

I shiver from the eruption.

She seeks. Wants to play.
She comes and I join her.

blue stars

Results matter. With or without nary a glimpse the sight of "why?" Ancestors, ancient and otherwise, placed eyes skyward. Saw heavenly body, set the worlds and worship to revolve around it: divine clockwork. And you tried. And you tried. And you tried, looking up, squinting until the tears obstruction. Boi you done fucked up again.

Hear tell once it was a soft thing, warm as summer lemons.

This though? Much brighter, a dense blue so bright it stabs through the corneas. Everything 'bout the legends seems off. Here there are no such saving rays, just an ultra violent glare, cold as the body of a girl whose fuel was spent in long eons past, whose body forgot to die.

tecumseh's invocation

Awaken and ready Oh Miami
the Big Knives even now array.
Their very body breathes
pestilence: an odd
auger of ill tiding.

I'd but six journeys 'round
the sun when the Big Knives
found Puckshinwa —still ecstatic
in their extinguishing
they renamed this sacred
soil Pleasant Point.

Puckshinwa who, at my birth –
placed the prophets portent
on the comets that blazed
that I might hunt,
might fight – might live
as a Shawnee son should;

At Mad River I, too, ran. Shame

found me before the musket
shells could. So at Wabash, Little
Turtle & Blue Jacket led.

It was the greatest of shows
I'm sure the ancestors saw.

Surely now Puckshinwa sits
smiling with the Great Spirit.
Surely now, they will leave, let us live.
I looked for more stars to shoot.
They were silent.
We must not forget: the Brits betray.

He-Who-Makes-A Loud-Noise
says: Big Knives kill Big Knives,
but never for long –
or the lifting of us.

We must become as
a loud door closing.

Let them hear the stomping
of charging feet. Cloaked
in the clothes of our people
let them hear the woop of our warcries

Sleep no longer! Oh
Chocktaw and Chickasaw, will not
the bones of our dead be plowed up
and their graves be turned to fields?

ozy

*"He who builds on the people, builds on the mud." –
Niccolò Machiavelli*

Behold! I did my damned thing
on the banks of a muddy muddy spill,
other side of a dirty delta. I deep dug
a little rock; built up boundaries
on embankments meant to make
a monument worthy
of remembering. They forgot

though. Callous fingers
and throat thrust into clay,
baked the bricks –
forged a foundation –
King of kings? I am become
a body of riddles only

the Sphinx retains.

arse: poetica

*"They all act right in the beginning,
it just those endings we always seem to
struggle through."* Some lovesick guy called
"Mo"

First time I saw her, she was
with her homegirls: Nikki, Sonia,
Rita, & Gwen. So fine!
She made each of them
sparkle sex and drip.

I wanted to feel her in me.

Y'all think it's sexy
the way she comes at night
begging, when all I wanna do
is race to diminishing – setting
like an old body at age.
She fights for me when
I am on my other shit.

Her and I been past that.
I'm an overdone almond,
but it wasn't always so
I used to go looking
for her. Meditate in the small
stillness and smile, imagining
what she looks like naked.
Only to find her filling up
some other sucker. Poly-
amorous hussy.

Y'all only see silver beams
and silhouettes in the sands,
always missing the broken bottles,
and husks of ships cracked like eggs,
empty as me. Y'all see the glint of translucent
waters waving but miss the warning: the flotsom
full of seamen, the aftermath of us all
once who raced, and swam, and died – begging
for her to be that blessing she was.

I used to jump up – beset, bewildered,
and bound: Samson to her Delilah
at the pear tree grinning at how she
done cut me off. Again. Back then I wouldn't
fight at all I'd rush in reckless and head long.
Y'all think struggle is romance.

The homies been done gave up on trying
to save this Black boy. Abandoned me
like blood after the shooting. They heard
the siren but don't see me trying.

Y'all never see how she done
destroyed every one who
ever tried to love her:
sent that freak Ovid to isolation,
drove Coleridge to the needle,
put the bourbon in Bukowski
and all we get in the end, maybe
are a few loved letters.

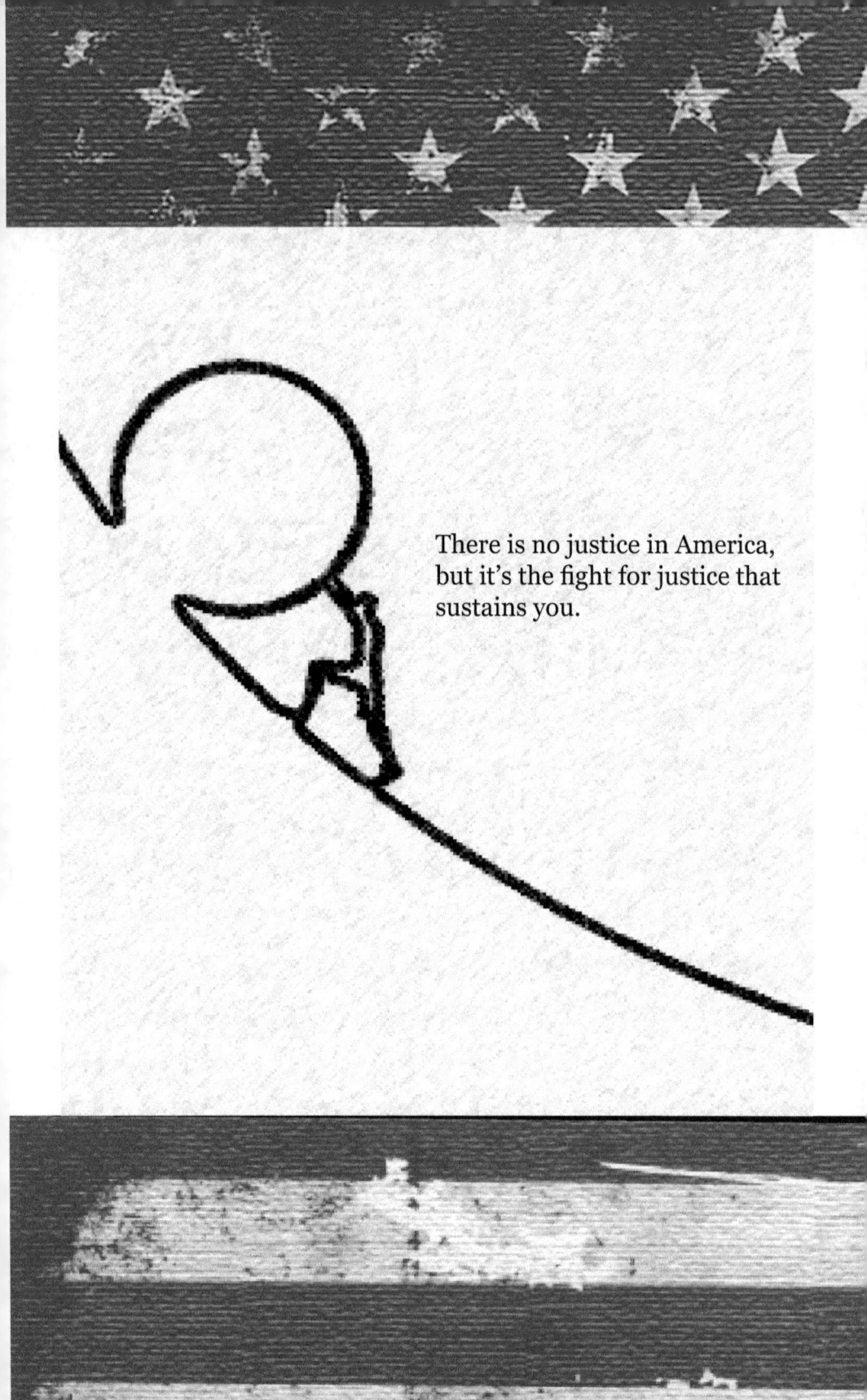

foibles

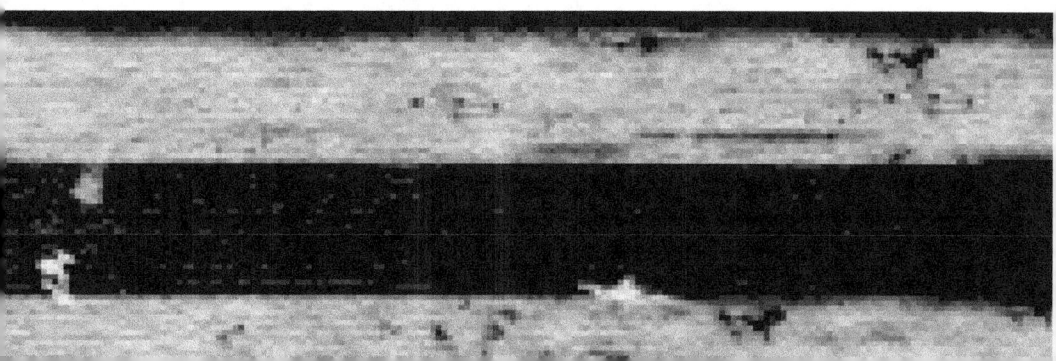

another round

They are at it again, upstairs – doors closed:
the continuation of commotion
that started in my room. Took turns with me.
Passed the belt like a blunt. Objectified

my ass, pants down, me all prayer and beg.
And me bent knees and bruised legs. And me: spent
powder keg. I go boom. Funny how forced
disciplining done turned quarrelsome mouths

into something much sexier. My bad
grades and half progress done forged a fucking
bond from a pair a scant few months away
from a failing of their own. Afterglow

Sullen, sore, swollen – I smell smoke, sneaking
out, better start my chores, before round two.

conductor

```
And 'lo there I                  Stood
in wonderous                     Awe
want-  ing            to         learn
to do    as    I      saw.

He looked through my
       Gleam

seeing   only    my              street.
Boldly told me    my teeth
were no good.     I     couldn't
blow flute, too short   for big        brass,
to − o poor
       for strings.
Played me smo − oth
       bent my
spirit like a           wrong note.
He waved his wand.      Made me
a dumb melo             dy out
of time. Ever
       y time.
A miracle                    of mus-
ic now, when I      look at
instruments my      stub- by
stubborn fingers    can    not
find the music             I      might
have made. If on-          ly I
had found anoth     er mag
ician of sound.
```

chrysalis

It's an empty, dried Brown
discarded thing. Crawled right
out of it. They was all
watching. Scorn dripping like
pus from my wounds – this what
that growth do. Leave you puf-
fy and raw. Never quite
so praised as before I
tried these new shapes, my kind-
a callous – corrosive:
courage aid for the Kool
sippers. It's wild taking
the armor off actu-
ally feeling what come
when the drip stops & di-
stills.

circus carnie

It was momma who taught
me how to throw em – daggers –
an easy enough trick.

First lock on a target – the you is implied.
Squeeze eyeballs into slits –
form them a jagged little glint.

Done right, the gaze
jellies the prey's resolve—
a tranquilizing venom

We ain't here to chase –
that's a trappers gimmick,
here we just throw death.

Any fool can squeeze
that tool and lay a body
low with lead. The skill

is to push an intention
past the point of skin –
here we train to cut.

Gaslight the volunteer
into fear's stillness
take the aim of our

enemy into full me-
asure with fat pointy
fingers that stab

air – preparing the target
for the words coming
out of our mouths.

the boy (after marie howe)

I don't feel as sorry as I should.

So far from the beginning of my failing
as a father – I forget

the eternities of when I was a dad
& not yet man

Glancing at boyhood, grabbing dinners
made of dine and dash, hoping not to catch a cramp
or a case

Somewhere on the other side of Arkansas

was a daughter, growing out her skin and words for
the first time

staying with that girl I married because we fucked
and came together, before we parted.

big timers, ar

Rob was still with us. Taz was there too.
Rob's cell released, back then, with the bell ring.
Back then, Taz padded up to showed heart

together they were gang and gridiron.
And there was a Serbian girl – Slavitsa
big as her Tercel, big as the body of the Rob

(whose big fists were small saucers)
big as the company they secretly kept.
Together they did it big. And there was

a big brother – Stojan, awkward
big hairy, a good 250 and still only
the fourth biggest in the double wide.

Then "the devil" snapped, attacked
himself: shot for the heart, survived
like a proper dumb Rock town

Black boy, us and them roaches:
it's wut we do. And I'm there, the least
of us all, broken as my overdrafts; hiding

from the wife I loathe: foisted
on me by the families I feared;
fucked – from a little pillow kissing

session a little less than safe.
And we are smiling, drinking
Vingac aged in Baltic oaks.

And Rob is swearing by the Blood,
with all them bullets he swiped
from Taz, still in his pocket.

Thinking about spending them
in a big way, on an out of pocket Wolf
street mother fucker that stay talking shit.

Slavitsa is cursing and giggling,
and flirting and dreaming big about ways
her and Rob will spend a life.

robbed twice

Nigger was out of pocket
so we popped 'em.

Big Rob fired first
Heckler and Koch provided the muscle
a new kind of porcelain God.

That boy became a body
cloaked in a fistful
of finger pull.
Naughty little target.

Death makes hard dicks of us all
or is it the killing? Time?

I was more fanciful   shot off zeros
                and one e-mail
                and a screenshot
                and some tweety tweets
tweeting 'bout some
learned White professor
Dr. Robert something or other
making a Sambo out of a lost
Negro not Nigger enough
to act the way he was 'posed to.

Robbed twice.

One got a life full of bars
the other got the wrath
      earned unemployment.
Earned a meritorious hatred of uppity ones.
      Earned an infamy good allies like him
were supposed to hedge against
      earned a shearing. Shed a sheeps coat.
We cut deep to the wolf blood runs
"read by everyone."

still

Girl I want you but I don't need you.

Joy feels like her drip
mapping a path down my throat
even when I choke
on her spirit the truth
of it is, she'll still –
find me smiling.

Girl I want you but I don't need you.

I get drunk on just the fumes:–
a wrong kind of urging
taught to me to yearn.
Her kind of love pickles
my liver. Too many times
have I let in just a little death–
a quaint kind of pimp.
I am a million hungry eyes.

Girl I want you but I don't need you.

She's on my walls, stacked
a centerfold who comes from every
where. I sell, when they come wanting.
Just like me, she got em all open
and puckered: sour cherry and bitter
amaretto. Her kiss filling the whole of a mouth.

dissolved girl

The doors open and we rush
to change hardwood into a plush carpet
of shag people. The peroxide tressed
lithe lively doll baby undulates
a provocation. I am 29 again –
for the first time.

Say it. Say my name.

The taint of sweet tobacco sours
her breath. Her eyes fall on me.
I heard her first –
something 'bout how she used
to strip to this band, back in the day.
We are all vibrating nostalgias:
except her Mr. Incel. He magics his hand

Shame, such a shame.

from manacle to razorwire;
manages to muscle the mimsy;
menaces himself to master his
mistress. Need a little love to ease the pain.
I ain't even tripping. Massive
Attack has taken to the stage.

Passion's over rated anyway...

dew of heaven

Homeward bound on a bump of bus
ride: her and I – a funny sight
to probing eyes. Unmistakable. A perennial
contrast: age, gender and skin.

Three little Black kids see us and giggle. Ever
the clever spy Talia scrunches, her face
and beams back a silly grin of sprite
and show: a puffy reverie – a bright bushy

prelude to a sleepful tease
of a peace – of happily ever
after – a fairy godmother
smiling to princesses.
She squeezes my hand: a blushing
fuel to the flush even
as she places the long of her
waves on my shoulders, winking to

the children who are antsy, still
watching her as she places a solitary
kiss on my cheek. She be high –
a helium pucker filling the fragile

of a latex balloon: wet enough
to spill
        a tear
or two onto my shirt.

She lays, and I am elated.

playlist she will never hear

I have homies. She has
some of the same. They can
all testify to about how I am a love
that can howl Ginsberg to blushing.
They sometimes sing similar
songs 'bout her.

This ain't bout them.

We used to trade songs:
 Sza "For The weekend," "Stealing Kisses" like little
Innocent Criminals. They say the first smiles
were warnings of teeth. Like affection –

This ain't about us.

She's the better song: a sunny
dipped contralto pitch-- a perfect
vibrato that can send a shimmer
straight down my stiff necked spine:
something to snap rhythm fingers to.
She'd call me "Big. Bad."
scatting it in four/four.

This ain't about her.
I want not to miss her, I do;
I want to tell her. I do
not. Longing is like fresh honey
drizzled on the caustic
of my tongue: a dope
I never refuse to shoot
and shout about.
I'm more, moody blues.

This is about me.
My throat – a scream of sad
that sours when sung. Even
now but a short distance
from the delta my sound can scare
the hell out of someone hearing
a Howling Wolf in the horizon.
When all I'm intent on is loosing a yelp
of an urge as material as the first
time I imagined her, wanting me.

This is about me.

legends and longing

The square's root always resolves
@ longing and I'm an armor clad adventure
boi – begging for a quest. Beset with a need
for her blessings. As good a failure as any

who ever tried. And here I am again, squinting
in the dark of this entrapment: shaped like a cave,
slick as her affections – wrapped in a honey do,
sliding into a hellmouth, trying to get to glory.

In lieu of the concrete of confession, I am
forced to finger my way through. Feeling for
the raw of a heat that doubles as guide, as proof,
as consolation. Here there are no answers

only a continuation of efforts as I Zatoichi
a beauty unbladed, a breaker of my bold.
Here there is only hope, and a fear of
resolution. For how could I dare envision

what form embodies the bringer of warmth?
How is the blind to intuit the intricacy
of difference between the sanguine
fanged Ryu and the sun?

as if (a fuckboi rebuke)

As if it was she that shed
                a bathtub of tough boy tears.

The phone will hum – flashing you
at an hour indecent as your sleeping
attire. There will be a string
of proclamations, of MYSM,
of "I was fucked up," of sorry you
had to deal, missing will be the real.

As if it was she that overdosed
                on anxiety

The Nigga that told her 'nah' must have
meant it, cause here she is throwing
corner dice; gambling on Pathos
providing a pardon for time served.

As if it were she
      who obsessed

over every note, every exchange, every
thing you ever shared. Trying to Sherlock
the flaw that walked her out your door.
She will dare to co-opt the cell

you sentenced you to. When she sends
<3 remember you are more. Polymorph
your mushy ticker into sterner stuff.

Be ribcage, be brick and mortar, be electric fence,
be gator stocked moat. Be turret, be munition, be
smart bomb, be strong enough to cry again. Be a
whole human. Be short, chubby, Jewish manboy.
Be-lieve you are worthy.
Be brave enough to
leave her ass on "read."

what i wanted

To be the small thing she loved –
one that wanted so hard
just to be one
of those good memories –

A smile tucked in the back
of a smirk in the back
of a grin in the back
of her head. Name on the tip
of a tattle like some swallowed little
secret thing.

And here I was again always
wanting way out loud – lapping
at her sticky drippy slow
drizzled love dangled
from some of the other tips
she spilled from –

grabbing into her vacuum
making cups of my palms –
trying so diligently to suck
what fell into my fingers
Addiction is the reach
that dumbs those that dare
dream of a taste that stays.

the offering

Ain't I a plucked pretty bird –
a posthumous feast for ravenous

nibblers. One bite please?
Didn't the bitties beg?

Didn't I consent – a shimmy
of color and show. Shook tail feathers

Didn't I strut, all pee and cock. Didn't I
dance for each and every tooth?

Didn't I dare them, come? Catch?
Didn't I coy, and coo and call? Didn't I

cry at every catch and release? Didn't I
dare damnation? Didn't I Capaneus?

Didn't I see the bolts flashing in their
irises? Ain't I picked – a clean

& culled husk? Didn't I smile tho?
Wasn't I happy? Wasn't I roasted

a plum and proper Thanks
giving for every open mouth.

& other
 'merican sins

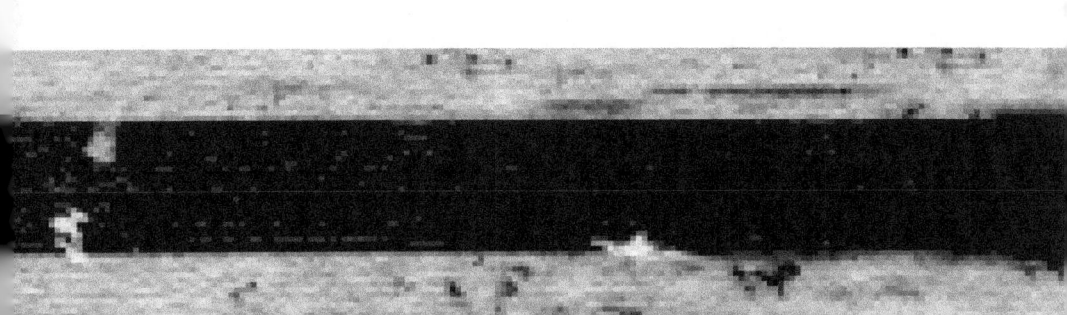

adjudication chamber

Do not go passive when you hear the guns.
Old age Black youth rarely earn.
Rage? Rage against the killing of our sons.

Though juried men fail us one by one
(worlds are changing) they'd see it burn.
Do not go passive. When you hear the guns

good people listen in: verdict stuns.
We're barely able to breathe – concerns.
Rage, rage against the killing. Our sons,

are little boys slug slain and slung hung.
It's 50's and Fonzies – A Happy Day's return.
Do not go passive when you hear the guns.

Grave men. Weep for the loss of Trayvon
he stood his ground (lessons learned).
Rage, rage against the killing of our sons.

And you America, fetid as a corpse becomes
left street dead in court's adjourn.
Do not go passive when you hear the guns.
Rage, rage against the killing of our sons.

carolina blood magic

Honored by staining skin into misborn artifacts, blood is the blemish bringer, dimpled freckled smile, life buried deep, betrayer of misborn secrets. Shit on the tips of tongues. The Frenchman dabbled in dappled skin. Some of his kin bore his name (some could bear the lash). Seed was for sowing, for bent Brown backs. Spread salvation! It's Jeffersonian kindness, task of good White men, an owner's burden. The yearning teacher's ritual.

Each stroke: a lesson in comeuppance for uppity
farm hands -- too tender to pick. 'Whollop the Nigger!' blood
moistens soil. Determination makes Denmark Vesey's.
Here when they run, we course bucks with coonhounds,
our Klan leaves 'em lay -- spilling, ruined like Golgotha.
We lay praying hallelujahs. Here blood means something.

language lessons

They asked us to speak English
smiling their war.
We heard it.

B L A C K. Adjective.

One:
        lacking hue and brightness;
        absorbing light without reflection
See why they slow?

Correction:
They are slow.
Speak properly. Like we told said!
Lack hue man.
We teach them anyway.
Mighty fine of you!
Christian.
White.

Two:
        characterized by absence of light;
        enveloped in darkness: a black night.

The hood is a lovely place
dangerous as doing the new thing.
Never spend money
(unless there's dope to cop)

How's that son of yours?
Just fine Jim! Already winking at the girls,
strong looker,
grins when he leans in for the punch.
Blonde as sunshine.

Three:
        Pertaining or belonging to any population characterized by dark skin pigmentation, specifically the dark-skinned peoples.

See also: African American

Sometimes capitalize initial letter.
optional as Oxford comma,
(mostly we forget)

You won't tell will you?
It's a White lie. Mighty Christian!!
God Bless you!

Four:
        soiled or stained with dirt:

Lazy, *always* begging.
Why won't they work?
See, I ain't a bigot or nothing but...
She likes 'em like that you know? Play's in the mud.
Some girls just don't respect their upbringing.
What would her grandmother say?

Five:
        gloomy; pessimistic; dismal: a black outlook.
        Blackmale. Blackheart. Blackmarket. Ha.
 Get it?
Look at that war raging. Why that boy so angry?
Why don't they ever smile?
I mean.
This is America.

peace be (for nikki)

That fine forebear say
peace be still
                                       looking.

Be blindboy in dead
alley on pitch night.

Peace be advertised
like xanax and war. Be
that sleep where the blood spill.

Peace be that thing
the boom brings

that bap on Brown backs.

Peace be missing
be deliberate as run aways marveling
at found food.
Be gone like girl
gone like desert rain
Gone like a past tense Felicia.

Peace be like AK spray,
like angry toddler
be mouthful of spit

Peace be compliance

and "get on the ground"
and" hands up."

Like DJ's and porkchops.
Forebear said Peace
was the beginning
and a whole word.
And we heard her.

We just still
       waiting
              for our piece.

We be looking for peace
like kind sounds from a Trump-
et, quiet as the death of a bomb-dropping
hater of unbent Saigonese.

Peace be that mellow to masculine.
       A detox and salve to smear
            upon bruised butted head.

Peace be that shame satiation that
     in similar situations
         we might sneer at.

I'm guilty too
     but I ain't the great "They"
so I'm that witness.
         Witness
              WITNESS.

Its not like we can't see.

Peace be locked up liquor store
      a crime to even get to
           a dirty job in and of itself.

Something we gotta want anyway. Still.

the key to hitting (for krit)

Jefferson's key to productivity: hitting
backs of Blacks. Virginia tobacco needs a hard
dark clay tilled with potash and long summer sun like
you couldn't even believe. The enslaved are a
pricey investment, and often disrespectful
breed, one must oversee like a proper stepdad.

Momma Hemmings said to never call him stepdad
or stare directly in his eyes: spare a hitting.
He look at Maw so lecherous: disrespectful.
I try just to pick leaves but forgetting is hard.
She ain't as young as she once was but he still a
ole ass man who be touching her in ways I'on't like.

Maw say my hair need cutting. Starting to look like
massa's texture under his wig. Skip a step. Dad's
bloody back is etched in whip patterns that paint a
pathway back to another land, a home. Hitting
is our only hope. Dear God, hoping hurts ~~this hard~~
and I think you not helping is disrespectful.

He hit me again. Says I speak disrespectful
He's crossed. Guess he see the Jesus Christ in me like
this burnt copper and kink shorn body blistered hard
exists only for the pleasure of my stepdad.
Maw saw him, and cried out. Now she's owed a hitting.
Moons a rising. Leading yoked oxen tilling a

patch of earth. Hoeing is laborious work. A
lot of things go wrong. Stony soil's disrespectful,
black cast iron goes dull until a sharp hitting.
Field hands seize moments: casting collars, running like

bucks. Running like men for office just like stepdad.
Running like oxen, running from whip. Running hard.

Ran like rivers hiding their scent making it hard
for the hounds to do their task. Noses sniffing a
snack for the nooses on the gallows for stepdad.
A Jeffersonian kindness: disrespectful.
People say your eyes pop, neck snaps and tongue bulges like
a gorged cock – drunk with the assumption of hitting.

Hitting hard. Hitting Maw disrespectful.
Him hitting dad hit me in the feels. It's a lot like
stepdad hits because he hates not hitting.

amber's song (with young ma)

Queen Shit! I carry – dick on my hips
and I'm quick with the clips. (Woop)
13 hours a day: I'm about my business.
"G" Shit. I got everything I need. But I
still need shit! Please cum over? She still
with you? I don't see shit. Do you want to touch?

Call the PoPo hoe! Call the PoPo!

Every problem needs a naming. Make me
Ms. Homicide outside! Shape me legal
Kick-door. Ms. Break-seams-like-Bad-Black-body.
Up in my space? (Woop) Get out the way. (Woop)
I keep a gun.(Woop) I shoot for fun. (Woop)
Show me your hands! (Woop)
Ask about me. Miss D.P.D. scion of Mr.
Lots-of-Black-friends and Mrs. Not-a-Racist.

Call the PoPo hoe! Call the PoPo!

Queen Shit. Call me Collector-of-hugs
or shedder of souls and no tears
or madam Hide-Motive-In-Black- Skin
Don't you try me! I do what you can't do.
I can walk out the back (woop)
I can shoot and not save you.

Call the PoPo hoe! Call the PoPo!

brown's legacy

"Fouding Fathers" are the school lunch
today. The patriotism was a bit salty
but the homies were bred on fatback
so we just added hot sauce
and slurped it down anyway.
John took eight years of spoonfuls and walked away hungry
for the flash of the D-boys,
'cause they were 'bout dat 'rithmetic,
and a little homie had to get paid. He lurks late.

The rest of us stayed
juxtaposed between firm expectations and indoctrination,
Between "I can not tell a lie", and "I have a dream"
between uniform day and my brother's passed down shoes.
High I.Q.'s mean little to attention starved kids on test day.
The homie Rob is an alarm startled eye. I am an empty belly.
Mike is field tripping acid,

We are a collective: failing.

Teacher does what she can
a mumble of breath & disappointment.
We bring her apples anyway,
(by way of confiscated smart phones).
The science lesson today was "matter".

We learned.
We don't.

boudin in goshen

"The Blood is the life." Leviticus 17

We're legendary fools with it for sho'
in them 'Gyptian swamps.
You should see em on a summer day
pig split and spilling all its secrets –
legs up to god like momma
after the sermon on special Sundays.

Muscle ripped straight
from the bone: drawn, quartered
and fired into rice stuffed casings
like a reprobate bullet in reverse.

The way we make
a mess of that meat! Surely
God wills it.

The best pigs are always served
smoked – it ain't kosher of course,
salt will fuck up your blood
pressure as surely as flinted lead.
God wills it.

Got 'em hot though. You
hear the siren's metal melody
over all the celebration?
Nicca's was saucin.

They must done seen
the blood wiped on our door
posts. We eat greasy

flesh with our fingers –
laced up, shoes on:
ready to go? Surely
God wills it.

Above the squeal and gnash
black helicopters shine
spotlights. Searching for one-two
lost souls – fuck 'em tho. We smile
but in the deep of our pit
we know in the mo(u)rning – many of us
will not see the sun's
next resurrection in Goshen.

expiration date

Show em them Scratch'd knuckle
bones scraped raw as heroin
off the plate – bloody as the needle.
I'm still needing. Show em fists up – a failed prayer.
Show em they're never gonna fuck with me again.
Why's it have to be this way?

The candyman called me
a junkhead. Can't see my Bruce:
told me to kick but showed this clown
an old balloon trick. I lost it laughing –
never gonna fuck with me again!
Show em – I'm fierce as this urging early
in the August AM. Show em the shells!
Casing the lane I seen him stay. Why's it have to be

this way? I keep my shit together.
No more dirty tricks. Just this buffet –
all I can eat. Shotgun? Show em –
rack this load. Slam it in his face.
Go ahead! Take the plunge in vain –
Never gonna fuck with me again...

who gets words

We all become poets
in our passing. Won't be many
allowed to speak at my home
coming. Few on this dirtspin
would even feel like a scrotum
drag here would be the thing to do.

Ta da it's a gathering of outlaws:

Justin's probably gripping
a bottle of bourbon
like a microphone
like a grudge. Fuck
even he wanted to swing on me
a time or two. We smoked
and smiled on it later.

Doug: cutest of the queer bois
can commemorate – I guess.
He was momma to them Ozark
mountains: a peg of the unholy
triumvirate. Jeni will be there
a mess of tits and tears.

In life ain't often a Black boy
gets to call his shot – to Babe
his Ruth. We get not near enough
minutes in the game to tell
our tail at will. Ask Will
if he woulda wished he could
"Run" it back:
make all y'all listen to
a broken Black boy
song one Mo 'gin.
In death, ash and dirt invoke

pause. All y'all here with me?
Cuban will be in the back
laughing and rolling something
unfuckwithable sticky.

Its gone be quite the time.
Moses will be at the door
chin checking haters –
keeping order in the name
of the Mo World. Don't
put yours on the other end of a
"Florida Man" headline.
Kita will cut whoever slips
by him, prolly best just
not to even try. Cause
we a bunch of wild ones.

Deathtime unlocks my cage
door in the most matter of fact
manner I may ever be. I ain't give
much of a fuck when I was breathing?
Don't make my specter make a spectacle,
Cause Young, I'll still show out.

>   Let me be the only boy
>   sad. Rejoice and touch something
>   soft if they're smiling and say
>   yes real loud. I promise I'm
>   wit' it. Bust 'em if you got em.
>
>   Inter me and stomp feet
>   make the world shake tectonic
>   until you smell the fear of those
>   on the outside of this thing of ours.
>
>   Let me be the only lie
>   in the room that day.

robert johnson's admonition
to scratch legba (at the crossroads)

In the darkest hole,
you'd be well advised
Not to plan my funeral 'fore
 the body dies,

Each time a renaming: Blues,
Color music, Rock & Roll
(That thing YOU do).

The soul was always mine,
a funky signature of
sound that reads
as ultraviolet notes
too low for you
to even register.

So take me and one day
find ya chi'llens fondling
my grooves , an aggressive beg
of egress only I can path.
I'll find them through their finger tips
and earholes

Trangression man
as you have taken
so do I distil
from too much flesh
down to black tar
all itch and addiction.

This, my royal benediction

I'll stick them: spill to fill the deep
of their emptiness.
Ya feel?

On the playback let my bright
never blind your eyes.

Blink hard and you'll miss.

Even now you're savvy of me
escaping all efforts
at containment of my contagion.
Your contracts,
your crossroads,
your caged hell will never hold.

My ears burn at every
missed appropriated note.
(Miscolored skin gives you away).

Trust I'll still be there
an anguiish of laugh at your Scratching –
still hissing a slither into vinyl –
delivering remembrance of the
gifts that can never go.

Hear a sound from a voice inside

This is how the Gods converse,
and your kinda magic
always had limits.

colophon

Myriad is a humanist sans-serif typeface designed by Robert Slimbach and Carol Twombly for Adobe Systems. Myriad was intended as a neutral, general-purpose typeface that could fulfill a range of uses and have a form easily expandable by computer-aided design to a large range of weights and widths.

Georgia is a serif typeface designed in 1993 by Matthew Carter and hinted by Tom Rickner for the Microsoft Corporation. It was intended as a serif typeface that would appear elegant but legible printed small or on low- resolution screens.

Recognized by Poetry Slam Inc as a "Legend of the South," Amoja Sumler is a nationally celebrated poet, essayist and one of the preeminent emerging voices of leftist intersectional social advocacy. A Watering Hole graduate fellow and MFA candidate Amoja's work throughout the Arkansas poetry scene was a legendary seed. From his essay's discussing the role of law enforcement to the value of capitalism he is best known for fusing the art of the intellectual into the familiar. Amoja has headlined poetry festivals such as the Austin International Poetry Festival, the Bridgewater International Poetry Festival, Write NOLA in New Orleans and Rock the Republic in Texas. As a resident artist of several southern Arts in Education rosters, Amoja lectures at schools and literary nonprofits, while teaching creative pedagogy and keynoting at social advocacy conferences like Long Beach Indie Film Pedagogy Conference and Furious Flower, throughout the nation.

www.ingramcontent.com/pod-product-compliance
Lightning Source LLC
Chambersburg PA
CBHW071318080526
44587CB00018B/3265